Hydroponics

The Green Thumb Guide to Hydroponic Gardening

Charlie Tucker

Hydroponics

© Copyright 2016 by Pinnacle Publishers, LLC - All rights reserved.

This document is geared towards providing exact and reliable information in regards to the topic and issue covered. The publication is sold with the idea that the publisher is not required to render accounting, officially permitted, or otherwise, qualified services. If advice is necessary, legal or professional, a practiced individual in the profession should be ordered.

- From a Declaration of Principles which was accepted and approved equally by a Committee of the American Bar Association and a Committee of Publishers and Associations.

In no way is it legal to reproduce, duplicate, or transmit any part of this document in either electronic means or in printed format. Recording of this publication is strictly prohibited and any storage of this document is not allowed unless with written permission from the publisher. All rights reserved.

The information provided herein is stated to be truthful and consistent, in that any liability, in terms of inattention or otherwise, by any usage or abuse of any policies, processes, or directions contained within is the solitary and utter responsibility of the recipient reader. Under no circumstances will any legal responsibility or blame be held against the publisher for any reparation, damages, or monetary loss due to the information herein, either directly or indirectly.

Respective authors own all copyrights not held by the publisher.

The information herein is offered for informational purposes solely, and is universal as so. The presentation of the information is without contract or any type of guarantee assurance.

The trademarks that are used are without any consent, and the publication of the trademark is without permission or backing by the trademark owner. All trademarks and brands within this book are for clarifying purposes only and are the owned by the owners themselves, not affiliated with this document.

Contents

Introduction	vi
Chapter 1: Introduction to Hydroponics and the Benefits	1
Chapter 2 : Growing Systems	6
Deep Water Culture:	6
Nutrient Film Technique:	8
Aeroponics	14
Wicking	16
Ebb and Flow	18
Chapter 3 : Growing Mediums	21
Chapter 4 : Lighting	25
Chapter 5 : Timers and Reservoirs	29
Chapter 6 : Understanding Nutrients	32
Chapter 7 : Understanding pH Levels	38
Chapter 8 : Temperature and Humidity	40
Chapter 9 : The Growing Process	44
Chapter 10 : Tips and Tricks to Ensure Your Success	48
Chapter 11 : Creating a Bubble Bucket	54
Material List	54
Shopping list for the local pet store:	54

The Building Process	54
Conclusion	76

Introduction

I want to thank you and congratulate you for downloading the book, *Hydroponics – The Green Thumb Guide to Hydroponic Growing*.

Hydroponics is one of the best ways to grow your own plants, vegetables, or flowers. Not only are you potentially providing yourself with fresh produce or flowers, but you are also participating in sustaining the earth and yourself. The use of hydroponics to grow plants can be dated back all the way to Egyptian times. Using hydroponics to grow plants allows for a much finer control over the environment your plant is growing in over soil, as well rids you of many problems that soil brings. Your plants will grow quicker in a hydro system, thus leading to quicker and larger yields.

Starting the process of setting up a hydroponic system and deciphering all of the different methods of growing can be very confusing and time-consuming. My ultimate goal in writing this book is to make the whole process much easier from start to finish for anyone who is just beginning. There are also tips and lessons to be learned for those who are already experienced with hydroponic growing.

Within this book, I will teach you all of the different hydroponics systems available, growing mediums, lighting types, the general hydroponic growing process, and much more! I've also included a step-by-step guide with illustrations to create your own hydroponic system at home.

Chapter 1: Introduction to Hydroponics and the Benefits

Hydroponics... To many veteran traditional gardeners, it may seem very confusing. There are thousands of websites that give you bits of information about hydroponics, about the process and about the benefits, but it seems that there are very few sources that give you all of the information you need.

With that being the case, it is no wonder that so many people are confused about what hydroponics is and how it works as well as the benefits of hydroponics.

I want to begin with what hydroponics actually is. Hydroponics is a system of growing food or other plants without the use of soil. It may seem a bit odd and you may be wondering how it is even possible, but it is my goal to prove to you that it is possible and it is actually better for you to eat these foods than those grown in the ground.

When most people think about growing plants using a hydroponics system, they think about plants that are suspended with their roots dangling into the water. This is a type of hydroponics system, but there are so many more systems, many of which are very easy to maintain and contain what are called mediums. We will talk about the different types of systems and mediums later in this book, but I feel it is important for you to know that it is very easy for you to find a system and a medium that works for you.

When you think about growing your plants in anything other than soil, you may be wondering where your nutrients will come from but the good news is that unlike when you grow your plants in soil, when you grow them in the nutrient rich solution, you are able to determine what nutrients go into your food.

Many people do not understand what the real benefits of hydroponics growing are; after all, it would seem that it would be easier to grow your plants in the ground and even more natural to do so but there are many benefits that I want to go over.

The first benefit is the fact that you do not have to worry about weeding your garden nor do you have to worry about pests in your gardens. No rabbits, raccoons, or other animals will be eating your food before you are able to pick it. You will not have to worry about bugs getting on your plants and killing them because the bugs come from the soil. With no soil, you will have no bugs, which means you will not have to use any pesticides.

Today, more and more people are becoming more aware of the way pesticides effect not only our food or our planet but also our bodies. Studies have shown that these pesticides can lead to disease and many health problems later on in life.

Studies have actually shown that these pesticides can lead to cancer, obesity, diabetes, Parkinson's disease, infertility, birth defects, and even autism. We are seeing more and more people suffering from all of these diseases than ever before in history and it all comes down to what we are putting on the food we eat.

Your plants are going to grow better than they do in soil. It may seem odd because we have learned throughout our lives that plants must have three things to grow, water, the sun, and soil, but when you use hydroponics, you are taking the soil out of the equation and it seems that it simply would not work. But this equation is outdated and it is time to learn how to grow our plants better.

The real equation should be water+sunshine+nutrients. In the past, the nutrients came from the soil, but now, your nutrients can actually come from the water. Our soil has been depleted of so many nutrients. No one rotates their crops any longer, they no longer allow their fields to rest every seven years, which leaves our food nutrient deficient.

When you grow your food in a hydroponics system, you are in charge of the nutrients your plants receive and you don't have to wonder if your vegetables have the nutrients they should. When you grow your plants in soil, you will find that the roots are very long. This is because the roots are seeking out nutrients. When you grow your plants in a hydroponics system, you will find that the roots are small, the plant is large and the fruit is much bigger than if you were to grow it in the ground. The reason for this is because the roots are not seeking out nutrients. Instead, the nutrients are brought to the roots. This allows the plant to use its energy to produce fruit instead of growing roots.

Space is another factor that many people consider when they decide to use a hydroponics system. Now, because of advanced hydroponics systems, you do not have to have a large yard to grow your own food. Hydroponics systems are great for growing a large amount of food in a very small space.

For those who are concerned about the amount of water used in the hydroponic system or are worried about polluting the environment, it is great to know that the water in the system is recycled and the system does not pollute the environment at all and hydroponics only uses $1/20^{th}$ the amount of water that traditional farming does.

When you use a hydroponics system, you will find that you will receive higher yields from your plants and the time between harvests is much shorter. This means that the total output from the plants is much higher than traditional farming techniques. For those who choose to sell some of their vegetables at farmer's markets and such, this can mean a lot more money is being brought in.

Growing with hydroponics is very easy to learn and understand and you do not have to have any prior knowledge to see great results.

Another benefit is that you can use recycled materials to create your systems. This means that you do not have to go out and spend a ton of money on your hydroponics system, but instead, you can use material you already have.

The food you grow is going to be high quality food. You will not only taste the difference when you eat it, but you will also feel the difference in your own body. This is because the food you are buying at the grocery store is nutrient deficient, however, your food will be full of vitamins and minerals.

On top of all of these benefits, you can turn your time gardening into time that you enjoy instead of another job that has to be done. Imagine what you would do with all the extra time. No longer will you have to pick bugs off of leaves, no longer will you have to dig through dirt trying to get the roots of weeds out of your garden or even worry about the plants getting watered every evening.

Whether you are a veteran gardener, a hobby gardener, or a new gardener, hydroponics has many benefits to offer you. If you are concerned that you will not enjoy hydroponics gardening, start out with a small system, plant some lettuce or berries, and chances are that during the next growing season, you will be adding a much larger system.

We have learned what hydroponics is, a system of growing plants without the use of water. We have learned about all of the benefits of hydroponics and how it can change your gardening life forever, but there is so much more about hydroponics that needs to be learned.

In the next chapter, we are going to go over the different types of systems that you can use when you switch from traditional gardening to hydroponics gardening. We will discuss each system in depth, allowing you to decide which system is best for you.

Chapter 2 : Growing Systems

There are many different types of hydroponics systems, deep water culture, nutrient film technique (NFT), Aeroponics, wicking, ebb and flow, and the drip system.

All of these systems are fairly simple; they are all systems that anyone can use and that do not take a lot of maintenance. I want to take this chapter through each of the systems in detail so that you are able to choose the best system for you and your lifestyle.

Deep Water Culture:

I want to start with the deep water culture system because it is the simplest of all of the hydroponics systems. This system is for those who only want to grow a small number of plants, is very cheap, and works well. However, it does take more maintenance than other systems.

The deep water culture system will rely on an air pump and an air stone, much like the one you would use in your aquarium, to keep the nutrient solution mixed as well as helping to generate the spray, which will get the medium wet, allowing the roots to establish in their net pots.

The water will have to be high enough in this system to saturate the medium, and this is usually done by the bursting of the bubbles caused by the air stone in the nutrient rich water. Once your plants have a good root system established, you will want to lower your water level, allowing the roots to hang in the air above the water level.

It is imperative that your air pump runs for 24 hours per day because if the roots dry out, for even the shortest amount of time, the plants will die and all of your work will have been for nothing. If the roots are left to sit in the water, they will become waterlogged, which will cause root rot, which will, again, kill your plants.

The good news is that you can use the material you already have around your house to create your deep water culture system. For example, a five-gallon bucket can be used to create a deep water culture system, but it is important for you to know you should only grow one plant per five-gallon bucket.

The reason for this is simply because if there are too many roots, they can engulf the air stone, which will cause a lack of aeration because of the root ball and this will result in the death of your plant.

Because this system does not depend on a reservoir, it is very important for you to ensure that the pH of the water stays consistent and often, this can take a lot of attention and time. We will talk about the pH of the water in a later chapter, but it is important for you to take this into consideration when you are choosing which system you would like to use.

Because your bucket is only going to be holding 3-4 gallons of water, you have to take evaporation into consideration as well. The water in your deep water culture is not only going to be absorbed by the plants, but it is going to evaporate as well, which means that there is a high risk of your plants not being able to get any water or nutrients after just a few hours.

For this reason, you want to be very careful about the amount of nutrients you put into your water. You see, as the plants absorb the water, they may not absorb the nutrients at the same rate, add into this, evaporation and your nutrient levels will become toxic to your plants very quickly. This means that you always want to put less nutrients in your system than in other system, in other words, you will underfeed your plants.

Because your water levels are going to fluctuate so much in your system, your pH levels will fluctuate dramatically, too. This means that you will have to put more effort into maintaining the correct pH levels of your water if you want your plants to survive.

This can cause many problems because when you are using this system, you will have to remove the lid, which means you will have to disturb the plant to check the pH levels and water levels.

If you have a small plant, lifting the lid and checking these levels is not going to be such a big deal because the root system will be very small but if you have a large plant, this could not only do damage to the plant itself but also to the roots, which, of course, could kill the plant. If you are using this system with large plants, you will also have to consider giving them extra support because the plants are grown in such a small amount of medium.

If you use the deep water culture system, you are going to have to check the pH levels and the water levels at least once per day. This means that if you are trying to maintain several of these buckets, with several different plants, you may find yourself with a full-time job just maintaining the systems. This, of course, is not what hydroponics is about so if you are wanting to grow more than one or two plants, you should consider using a different system.

Nutrient Film Technique:

After reading about the deep water culture system, you may not feel that permaculture is right for you, but I want to share a bit about the Nutrient Film Technique or NFT. This system is fairly easy to set up and operate, it is fairly simple to grow your plants in this system and it is very easy to replace your plants after you have harvested, which will provide you with a nonstop supply of healthy produce.

The best plants for an NFT system are those that are small and grow fast. Kale, lettuce, mustard greens, oriental vegetables, and many herbs can be grown in the NFT systems, and the great news is that all of them can be grown in the same system at the same time.

The nutrient film technique system will have a thin layer of nutrient rich film that flows over the roots of the plants. There is very little medium used, the only one being the small piece that the seed is started in. This medium is necessary only because if the seed is not sown in the medium, it will float away and get lost in the rest of the system.

Your plant's needs will be met through the air and the water solution that is washed over the plant's roots. The nutrients and soluble fertilizers are dissolved in the water, which will circulate through the system and supply the nutrients and minerals necessary for the plants to grow.

Your plants will also need lights. The best place for your system is in a small greenhouse, however, if you have a window that is facing the south or enough artificial lighting, that will work for this system as well.

Your plants will be grown in small channels that are flat on the bottom, but are positioned on a slope so that the nutrients are fed into one end and drained and collected by the reservoir tank at the other end. You can also use a return pipe to collect the water and return it back to the reservoir tank. The amount of slope will be between 1% and 3%, depending on how long the channels are. You will determine the length of your channels by the amount of plants you want to grow, but they can be as small as 2 feet long and as large as 15 feet, which is the size of channels used in commercial growing systems.

You do not want channels longer than 15 feet because they cause many different problems, one being that they are very hard to move in the system, the plants at the end of the channels often do not grow well because all of the nutrients have been depleted once the film reaches these roots.

Most channels will be set up parallel of the greenhouse using 90° angles at the corners of the greenhouse and the system usually runs the entire border of the green house. The reason for this is that the NFT system will not take up a lot of space in your greenhouse if you set it up this way, which will allow you to use the rest of the space instead of it all being taken up by the one system.

There are many different types of channels available for you to purchase from hydroponic system and equipment suppliers, but many people simply choose to use PVC pipe.

Although some people love using PVC pipes, there are some disadvantages to using the pipes in this system. The first disadvantage is that the bottom of the pipe is rounded. This means that it does not create an even layer of nutrient rich solution and that some of the roots will become waterlogged while others will get no nutrient solution at all. This, of course, means that the plants are not going to grow consistently and it can often cause your plants to die.

However, this does not mean that these types of pipes will not work at all for this system, it simply means that it is not going to produce as high quality plants as you would get if you used a channel that was made specifically for this system.

Another issue with PVC pipe is that if it is exposed to light, specifically UV lights, for a long time, it will become very brittle and will break. NFT Channels that have been created specifically for NFT systems are created using a compound that protects against UV light. These channels will last much longer than PVC pipes when they are exposed to UV lights or when they are in a greenhouse.

Another disadvantage of using PVC pipes in your NFT system is that there is a lot more work involved because you will have to drill holes in the pipes to hold the plants. This can take a lot of time if you are trying to create a larger system. You will also have to ensure that the table you are using to support your system is designed in a manner that ensures the pipes are not able roll or shift your plants and that your nutrient rich solution is not able to leak out of the pipes.

Cleaning the channels between crops can be very difficult if you use PVC pipes for the channels, however, channels that have been specifically created for NFT systems are much easier to clean.

You have to clean the channels because fertilizer and nutrients can build up inside of the channels, collecting on the sides, and there is enough light in the channels to allow algae to grow. This has to be cleaned out of the channels, each time the plants are harvested and before the next set of plants are introduced.

The next part of the NFT system is the reservoir. This is where the water and nutrients will be held when they are not flowing through the system. The nutrients and water will return to the reservoir after it has run through the system and the process will begin over again. A simple plastic container is sufficient for a reservoir, as are heavy duty garbage cans and watering troughs that have been designed for livestock.

It is important to remember that galvanized steel or other metal containers should not be used. This is because these materials are reactive, the fertilizer is corrosive to these containers, and they can cause part of the material from a metal reservoir to be transferred into the system, which can destroy your plants.

You will determine the size of your reservoir by the number of plants you plan on growing. For every 40 plants, you should have a minimum of a five-gallon reservoir. You should also add another gallon to your total for every 20 heads of lettuce you are growing.

It is important to remember that it is much better to have a reservoir that is too large rather than too small. It is also important to remember that on warmer days, the plants are going to need more water than on cooler days and to adjust your reservoir according to that fact.

Because the plants are going to need much more water on warmer days than on cooler days, you need to remember to reduce the amount of fertilizer and nutrients you are putting into your solution because it can reduce the growth of the plants and even kill them.

Next, you will need a re-circulating pump that is large enough to keep the solution pumping through the system. The pump has to be designed for corrosive material because of the corrosiveness of the solution, a simple, non-corrosive pump will be fine for your system.

A small NFT system can use a fountain pump and have no issues. If you are using a fountain pump, you need to make sure that the highest point of your channels is no more than 3 feet above the infeed end of the NFT system.

It is always better to have a stronger pump than what you have to have rather than one that is not strong enough to handle your system or one that is barely able to handle your system.

The capacity of the pump is listed on the packaging and you need to look for a pump that will pump about five times the number of gallons of nutrient solution needed per hour. This is because you want to make sure your plants are getting the right amount of nutrients from the solution and that the solution is able to make it to the end of the channels and back to the reservoir.

It is advised that you purchase a timer that can be connected to the end of your pump plug before you plug it in. This will ensure that your plants are getting the nutrients they need while not becoming water logged or getting root rot from being left in a channel of continual water.

If you do not want to use a timer, using a pump that is stronger than you have to have will allow you to circulate the solution continuously through your channels.

You will need irrigation lines and emitters for your NFT system. You will need poly pipe that is used for irrigation to bring your nutrient solution from your pump to your emitters, which will deliver the solution to each of your channels.

Poly pipe is going to allow you to insert your emitters directly into the pipe without having separate connections. It will also allow the emitter to be placed where ever you need it along the poly pipe. You will want to get flexible poly pipe because if you use rigid PVC pipe, you will not be able to place your emitters where you need them.

You will want to use non-pressure-compensated emitters when you have a small NFT system and are using a small fountain pump. These types of pumps do not produce the amount of pressure needed to ensure a uniform delivery of your nutrient solution, and this is why you will use this type of emitter.

You will rarely use a pressure compensated emitter even in a large system because your pump should be large enough to create the pressure needed and a pressure compensated emitter will only be an unnecessary expense.

Finally, you will need a drain line. The drain line is going to catch all of the nutrient solution after it has moved through the channels and it will return it to the reservoir where the solution will be re-circulated throughout the system. You can make your drain pipe out of 4 inch PVC pipes and the fittings for the pipes. Many growers choose to use Polyethylene drain line because it is black on the inside while white on the outside, which reduces the chance of any light getting into the pipe and ensures that algae growth cannot be supported. It will also ensure that the water in the pipe does not get too hot because the white outside will reflect the light instead of absorbing it. The way you cut your drain line will depend upon how you design your system.

Aeroponics

Aeroponics is another hydroponic system that you can use to grow your plants. Instead of using soil to grow your plants or a medium, you will use air. The system works by suspending the plants in a dark grow bed and they are periodically sprayed with a nutrient rich solution.

I am not going to go into a ton of detail about Aeroponics because although it is considered a hydroponic system because there is no use of soil, there are many different systems that can be used in Aeroponics and those are a completely different topic than what we are discussing.

Aeroponics systems are not difficult to use and many people have a lot of success when it comes to growing their plants. The system allows the plants to grow much faster and produce more just like the other hydroponics systems, but the plants will require much less nutrients and water than other hydroponics systems will.

In most cases, you will suspend your plans over a reservoir within a sealed container, feeding the plants though a pump and sprinkler system that will periodically spray the solution onto the roots of the plants.

However, there are a few problems with this system. One is that if your timer breaks while you are gone to work, all of your plants will quickly die and chances are you won't get to them in time to save them. The same thing will happen if the electricity goes off. This system is very dependent on the timer and without it, the system will collapse in a few hours.

The other issue is that because the roots are kept in an environment that is continually wet, they are susceptible to the growth of bacteria, which can spread through the system quickly. If the roots are kept too wet, they will rot and if they are not wet enough, your plants will die. Finally, this system can get very expensive. You will find that you are replacing your parts often, you will need to keep a few pumps on hand, and if you plan on going on vacation, you will need someone to take care of your system and make sure that it is running properly.

Aeroponics is a great way to grow your plants in a small space and to ensure that you are growing healthy vegetables, but many people find that it is simply too stressful to maintain this type of system.

Wicking

Wicking will allow water to travel up to your plants without the use of pumps simply because of the wicking action. You can use many different types of medium in a wicking bed and we will talk about these later in this book, but the purpose of the medium is to absorb the water, bringing it up to the roots of the plants while ensuring that the roots do not become waterlogged.

The wicking system is one of the easiest of all of the hydroponics systems and that is because it does not have any moving parts or pumps, and as such, it does not need any electricity. Some people do like to use an air pump in the reservoir to keep the nutrient solution mixed and to ensure there is enough oxygen in the water.

Because this system does not have to have electricity to work, it is a great way to grow plants using a hydroponics system in an area where there is no electrical plugs or where the electricity is unreliable.

This is a very simple type of system to use and is one that many people choose to use when they are first learning about hydroponics as a way to get their feet wet before moving on to more complicated systems. Many teachers will use this type of system in their classrooms as a way of getting their students interested in hydroponics.

When you are creating a wicking system, you will need a container for the plant, a larger container for the reservoir, a wicking medium, and a second wicking medium that is in the form of strips or ropes.

The wicking system operates in just the same way it sounds. It simply wicks up the nutrient rich solution from the reservoir, bringing it to the roots of the plants. Most good wicking systems will use at least two mediums, ensuring that enough water is brought to the roots of the plants.

The container that holds your plants will sit just above the container you are using for your reservoir. This will ensure that the water does not have to travel far to get to the roots of the plants.

One of the downsides to the wicking system, and probably the biggest, is that they work best with smaller plants because the larger plants have to absorb more water. This system is much better suited for small plants, for example, herbs and lettuce, and it is best for plants that are non-fruit bearing.

While the wick will suck up the water for the plant, bringing the moisture to the roots, the bigger the plant is, the more water it will need and the harder it will be for the medium to bring enough water to the plant.

Fruit bearing plants must have a lot more water than those that do not bear fruit and for the same reason as above, you do not want to grow them in a wicking system. If you try to grow a fruit bearing plant in a wicking system, you will have small fruit that lacks vitamins and nutrients.

Another downside of the wicking system is that they are less effective at delivering the nutrients to the roots of the plants. This means that plants that require very heavy feeding will not do well in a wicking system. Lettuce and herbs and kale are not heavy feeders while other plants, fruit bearing plants, are the heaviest feeders.

Finally, the last downside is that most plants in a wick system will not absorb water or nutrients evenly because the wick has no way of telling what nutrients the plant needs. The plant simply takes the nutrients and water it needs from the growing medium and leaves the rest. This means that some of the nutrients can build up and cause a toxic environment for the roots. To avoid this, you will have to rinse the excess nutrients out of the medium with fresh water at least once per week.

The wicking material or medium is the most important part of this system because without a good wicking material, the water and nutrients will not be able to get to the roots of the plants.

You will probably want to do some experimenting with the different types of medium you use for the wicking in your system so that you can find the best wicking medium for your system.

The Reservoir

Your reservoir can be a large one or a small one, but you want to make sure that it does not become dry at any point. You also want to ensure that the water level is high enough so that the nutrients do not have to travel far up the medium to get to the roots. It is important for you to fill the reservoir with nutrient solution as it depletes and you will need to clean out the reservoir on a regular basis as well, completely changing the nutrient solution.

You need to do this because algae and other bacteria will be able to grow in the reservoir. If the algae grows in the reservoir, it will absorb the nutrients you want your plants to absorb.

Ebb and Flow

The ebb and flow method is one that is well known for its reliability, the low cost, and its simplicity. The flood tray is filled with a grow medium, but it is important to know that these do not work in the same way soil does. The medium does not provide nutrients to the plants, but they will work in the same way as soil when it comes to anchoring the roots of the plants. The medium will also temporarily hold the water and nutrients, allowing the roots to absorb them before the nutrient solution is drained back into the reservoir.

Your flood tray will need to be flooded between 4 and 6 times per day, and the flood tray should slowly drain in between floods.

With the ebb and flow system, the flood tray will contain a medium that will be periodically flooded with a nutrient rich solution. You will place the flood tray over the top of the reservoir so that gravity will work in your favor. After your pump stops flooding the flood tray with nutrients, the solution will naturally drip back into the reservoir and the process will start all over again.

Aeration is one of the most important things when it comes to the ebb and flow system. The reason for this is because when the plants are not flooded, they are able to absorb the amount of oxygen they need, but when they are flooded, they only oxygen they can absorb is what is in the water.

When you use an ebb and flow system, you will also find that the air pump is going to help keep the nutrients mixed into the water. Many people think that just because the water is continuously flowing through the pump, it will stay mixed well, but nutrients have a bad habit of sinking to the bottom of the reservoir and if this happens, your plants will not get the nutrients they need.

Of course, just like with any other system, there are a few drawbacks when it comes to the ebb and flow system (also known as the flood and drain system). The first drawback is that bacteria and algae are going to grow very quickly in the reservoir in this system. This is because the top of the reservoir is uncovered, allowing the nutrient solution to drain back into it after the flood tray has been flooded. Of course, as we have already learned, when algae grows in your reservoir tanks, it takes the nutrients away from the plants.

The other drawback is that there is a limited amount of oxygen available to the plants when they are in flood stage and as they are draining. The last drawback is that the system does rely on pumps and electricity. This, of course, means that if your pump goes out, your flood tray is not going to be flooded, which means that the roots of your plants will dry out very quickly.

Those are the most popular types of hydroponics systems that are used by growers today. Each of these systems has its downfalls and each of them have their perks, but it is up to the grower to choose the best system for them.

Chapter 3 : Growing Mediums

In the last chapter, I talked a lot about the mediums that can be used in your different hydroponics systems. In this chapter, I want to go into more depth about the different mediums you can use and what systems they work best in.

Rockwool is a sterile, non-degradable medium that is porous and is composed of granite or limestone. The granite or limestone has been super-heated, then it is melted and finally spun into threads so that it looks almost like cotton candy. After the Rockwool is spun into threads, it is formed into blocks, slabs, flocking, cubes, or sheets. Rockwool is great for sucking up water, but you have to make sure that it does not become completely saturated or it will drown your plants. This makes it a great medium for wicking systems, but it is important for you to balance the pH of the Rockwool before you use it in your system. The way to balance the pH of the Rockwool before putting it into your system is to simply soak it in water that is pH balanced before you place the Rockwool in your hydroponics system.

Grow Rock is expanded clay that is lightweight and has been super fired. When the clay is super fired, it creates a porous texture. The grow rock will allow your plants to secure their roots, but it is still considered light weight. Grow rocks do not degrade or dissolve so they can be used over and over. They are a sterile medium, they hold moisture, and will also work as a wick in wicking systems. The grow rocks are pH balanced so you do not have to worry about them affecting the pH of your water. When you are ready to clean your system and start a new season of crops, you can simply clean and sterilize the grow rocks before using them again. This can take a lot of time, but it is worth it when you consider the price of a medium. Grow

Hydroponics

rock is a very popular medium that can be used in most systems that require medium and this means that any store that sells hydroponics supplies should have grow rock.

Coco Fiber and Coco Chips are both formed from the outer coconut husk. This husk was once thought of as waste, but it has been found to be one of the best growing mediums to date. Even though the chips and the fiber are organic material, they both decompose very slowly, which means that they will not add any nutrients to your nutrient rich solution. Both the chips and the fiber are pH neutral, so you do not have to worry about balancing the pH nor do you have to worry about it affecting the pH of your nutrient solution.

The only difference between the chips and the fibers is their size, which means they are very versatile when it comes to using them in your hydroponics systems. For example, the chips will allow for air pockets to be in between them, which will allow for aeration in the roots. The fiber is great to use in wicking systems with other mediums such as grow rock.

Perlite is an organic material that when it is popped, expands and becomes very light weight. It is also porous and very absorbent. Perlite is used in potting soils and is, in fact, the small white balls that you will find in your potting soil. You can purchase it at a nursery but because it is also used in cement, it may be cheaper for you to purchase it at a building supply store.

You want to make sure that you rinse the dust off of the perlite before you use it in your hydroponics system and you will want to wet it while you are working with it so that you do not inhale the dust off of the perlite.

Vermiculite is a mineral that is much like perlite in that it is expanded when it is heated at a very high temperature. The vermiculite is different from perlite because it can hold nutrients for later use. Like perlite, vermiculite will float. It is used for very specific uses and it is best if you talk to your nursery before you choose to put this in your hydroponic system.

Oasis cubes are much like Rockwool cubes, but they are more rigid and are often used in floral displays. They are also called open cell material because the cells are able to absorb water and air. This allows the cells to be used in wicking systems because they are able to wick the nutrient solution to the roots and allow them to grow through the cell's structure

These cubes are great to use as starter cubes when you are using a hydroponics system, but they also come in bags, which will allow you to fill your grow containers with the oasis cubes. Although they are like Rockwool cubes, unlike Rockwool cubes, they will not become waterlogged; however, this does not mean that you should allow them to stay in contact with the water supply at all times because you will still have issues with root rot and water logging.

Floral foam is another material that can be used as medium in a hydroponics system because it is much like the oasis cubes. The cell size of the oasis cubes is much larger than the floral foam but it will allow you to design how you want to use the foam in your system. However, there are a few issues with floral foam, one being that it crumbles very easily and this can lead to you having particles in your water and it can become waterlogged if it is left in contact with the water on a constant basis.

Grow stones are a medium that is made from glass that has been recycled and are very similar to grow rocks. The stones are light in weight, porous, unevenly shaped, but they are also reusable and provide great aeration to the roots. The grow stones are also reusable, have the ability to wick water up to 4 inches, but it does need to have good drainage to ensure that it does not wick the water up all the way to the top. If you allow the medium to stay wet, it can cause root rot. Some people are concerned that because the medium is made out of glass, it will cut the roots, but you do not have to worry. The stones are not sharp and will not become sharp even if they were to break.

Of course, there are many other mediums that can be used in your hydroponics system besides the ones we have covered in this book, but I hope that this chapter has given you a few ideas of what types of medium you can use in your hydroponics systems.

Chapter 4 : Lighting

This chapter is going to cover the basics of lighting for your hydroponic system. Of course, you can use natural lighting, placing your outdoor hydroponics system on the south side of your house, but in this chapter, I want to cover artificial lighting.

One of the most important things you need to learn about when you are learning about growing with hydroponics, besides the actual system, is the lighting.

If your plants do not receive the light they need, they are not going to grow properly nor are they going to produce the amount of fruit you want. To become the best grower, you always want to find out what is limiting you the most. Learning what is limiting you the most and learning as much about it as you can is going to allow you to increase the growth of your plants without adjusting anything else.

When you think about lighting, you have to realize that no matter how great your system is, no matter how great the medium you are using is, no matter how high the quality of your fertilizer, without the proper light, your plants will never be able to grow healthy, strong plants.

The first thing you have to know about is the color of light that your bulbs produce. You see, every bulb will produce a colored light that is measured in degrees Kelvin; this is how the hue produced by the bulb is specified.

Most plants are going to grow better with a bulb that is 6500° degrees Kelvin. Flowering plants, on the other hand, are going to grow better at 2700k degrees Kelvin.

Of course, there are many different variables that will affect the rate at which your plants grow, but the most

Hydroponics

important of these variables is light. Using a high quality light is the only way you can guarantee your plants will grow to their fullest potential.

There are a number of lighting systems on the market today and each of these systems have their own pro's and con's that need to be taken into consideration, but it is important for you to remember that choosing the correct lighting for your indoor growing is the most important thing you can do to ensure effective growing.

Incandescent lamps are the first of the lighting systems that I want to talk about. These are what are known as the standard household light bulbs, and they are not very efficient when it comes to growing plants. They actually only have about a 5% efficiency rate. Incandescent lamps are not recommended for growing plants.

Fluorescent lights are a great choice if you are planning on growing your plants indoors. The best fluorescent lights are high output lights, which are about 7 times more efficient. This simply means that the lights will put out more light while using less electricity. A wide range of spectrums are available when it comes to fluorescent lamps and the 6500k are the best for indoor growing.

If you are growing larger plants, using fluorescent lighting is not advised as these are better for smaller plants. The fluorescent lamps are not as good at penetrating as the high intensity discharge lamps are.

There are many options for growing plants when it comes to fluorescent lights. You can choose lights that will be hung above the plants or that are hung to the side of the plants.

Another very popular form of fluorescent lights are the compact fluorescent lights or CFLs. These were designed as an alternative to the normal household bulbs or incandescent lights because they use less electricity and are supposed to have a longer life than incandescent bulbs. The CFL's are good for growers who are on a small budget and are growing small plants.

The great thing about CFLs is that you do not have to worry about the wiring, they don't require anything more than a standard socket, and they are extremely low in price. If you are going to use CFLs, you should consider using a reflector of some type, otherwise you will be wasting a lot of light that you could be using for your plants.

High intensity discharge lamps are the next type of lighting that I want to talk to you about. Also known as HID, these bulbs are the top pick for most growers. These are usually the types are generally used in street lights, parking lots, and warehouses. These lights are the top pick for today's growers because their output is 8 times more efficient than regular household light bulbs.

Light emitting diodes or LEDs are some of the new technology that growers are using for their plants because they use much less electricity than the other light sources mentioned.

There are many different things you need to think about when you are choosing your lighting. Your budget is the first thing that you need to think about when you are choosing your lighting for your hydroponics system. Those who are working with a low budget will be better off using T5 fluorescent tubes as will small scale growers.

If you have a large budget, the HID lamps are the highest quality, but you will need to consider getting them their own ventilation system because they will significantly raise the temperature of the room otherwise.

LED lights are great for those who are going to be growing for a long period of time because they will save you a ton of money on your electric bill. For example, some growers save as much as $5,000 over the lifetime of their LED bulbs.

Of course, this is just an example and it all depends on the price of electricity, how much you are willing to invest upfront, how often you use the lights, the type of environment the lighting system will be in, and so forth.

Once you have chosen your hydroponics system and your medium, you will need to spend some time thinking about the type of lighting system you will be using. It is important to remember that the lighting system is the most important factor when it comes to growing your plants indoors and it is not something you should take lightly.

Chapter 5 : Timers and Reservoirs

Some of your hydroponics systems, such as the ebb and flow system, will require a timer to be put on them to ensure your plants do not dry out. These timers are very simple to attach to your system and the easiest timers will simply attach to the plug at the end of your pump.

You will simply choose the amount of time you want your timer to be off between filling your flood tanks and how long you want your pump to be on. It really is that simple when it comes to your timer. The good news is that you do not have to have anything fancy; size does not matter and you don't have to spend a lot of money on your timer.

Reservoirs are also a part of your hydroponics system that you do not have to spend a lot of money on. The first thing you need to think about when it comes to your reservoir is the size. As a good rule of thumb, you will need ½ a gallon of nutrient solution per small plant, you will need 1 ½ gallons of water per medium sized plant and 2 ½ gallons of water per each large plant.

These numbers are minimums. You do not have to worry about getting a tank that is larger than what you need, but you do need to make sure that you do not go overboard when it comes to size because you will be wasting a lot of your nutrient solution. The good news is that you do not have to fill your reservoir up all of the way until the plants are larger or until you place more plants in your grow beds.

No matter what the size of your reservoir, you need to make sure that you mark the inside of the reservoir with a permanent marker at different levels. You should mark the gallon levels, for example, 1, 3, 5, and 10 gallons. This will help ensure you know where your water is supposed to be and the amount of water your system is using.

There are also environmental issues you want to take into account when you are thinking about your reservoir. Humidity is a huge factor when it comes to how much water your plant will need. The less humidity that is in the air, the more water your plant will need. If the plant does not get enough water, the plant will go limp and will eventually die.

As you would expect, as the heat rises, your plants will need more water. Some plants are able to tolerate more heat than others, but you should always keep an eye on the water levels when the temperature begins to rise.

There are different types of reservoirs can be made out of many different types of materials, many of them can be made from material you have at your home right now. Many people choose to make their reservoirs out of plastic totes, garbage cans, or animal troughs. It does not matter what you make your reservoir out of as long as you do not make it out of a metal container because these are corrosive and will leave bits in your nutrient solution. The one thing that does matter, however, is that you take care of your reservoir.

You need to make sure that it is cleaned on a regular basis, that algae is not allowed to grow in the tank, that the pH levels are balanced, which we will discuss in a later chapter, and that the water is not continuously on the roots of your plants.

Reservoirs are very simple; most of them are simple to maintain and very simple to build, even if you are making them on your own. If you do not want to make them on your own, you can purchase them at your local garden store. One thing that I have found is very important is that you paint the outside of the reservoir white and use black plastic on the inside of the reservoir.

The reason for this is because the white will reflect the light off of the reservoir and the black will reduce the chances of algae growing in the reservoir.

Chapter 6 : Understanding Nutrients

Because you are not using soil to ensure that your plants are getting all of the nutrients they need, you are going to have to provide these nutrients for your plants. This means you are going to have to use what is called a nutrient rich solution.

You will have to ensure that your nutrient rich solution contains the proper nutrients for your plants and that the nutrients are delivered to your plants effectively. This is the only way to ensure optimal health for your plants. We have already talked about the different systems you can use to deliver the nutrients to your plants, but up until this point, we have yet to really discuss the nutrients.

Again, the nutrients are a very important part of your hydroponics system because if you get the nutrient rich solution right, you are going to be rewarded with lots of healthy plants. However, if you get the solution wrong, you are going to face poor yield and possibly the death of your plants.

The solution must contain the correct nutrients, and the correct amount of nutrients and other minerals that are found naturally in the soil. Each of these nutrients is vital to your plant's growth, to ensure it does not suffer from disease and that it is able to continue to grow even if pests do get to part of the plant.

The first thing that you need to think about when it comes to your nutrient solution is the water you are going to be using. Most people are able to use normal tap water, however, you need to check the pH levels of the water (we will discuss pH levels later) and determine if they are manageable. You also need to consider the chemicals that are in your water.

For example, a person who lives in an area where they drink well water generally does not have to worry about the chemicals in the water because the well has been dug directly into a spring. This water is untreated. However, those who have highly treated water, that smells of chlorine or contains a large amount of fluoride or other chemicals, will want to consider using a different source for your water.

If you do not know how many different chemicals are in your water, you don't have to worry. As long as there is not a large amount of chemicals in the water, you can fill your reservoir 24 hours before you plan on mixing your nutrients, allowing the water to sit and you will not have to worry about the chemicals. This is because most of the chemicals will evaporate within the first 24 hours.

However, if you know that you need to drink bottled water where you live, you can smell the chemicals in your water, or the water in your city is known to make visitors sick, it is advisable for you to find a different source for your water (for example, gallons of drinking water, that is purchased from the store, can be used in your system).

Even if you are not worried about the amount of chemicals in your water, if you allow the water to sit in the reservoir for 24 hours before mixing your nutrients, you will be able to calibrate your pH levels more easily. If you are still concerned about the water you are using in your system, you can collect rain water and use it in your hydroponics system to ensure that your plants are getting the freshest water possible.

Because plants prefer fresh water, you should make sure that you will be able to drain and replace the water in your system once per week. This will also ensure that the water does not become stagnant and will allow you to clean your reservoir each week, which will ensure that there is no algae growing in your reservoir.

Your pH levels are going to fluctuate every day or every couple of days, so it is important to keep an eye on this. Some fluctuation is okay, but too much can kill your plants. We will discuss how to keep your pH levels balanced later on in this book.

Flushing your system out once per week with new water can mean all of the difference when it comes to the amount of crops you are able to harvest. We will talk about how you can adjust your pH levels in between flushing your system later on in this book and why it is important.

There are many different types of solution for your plants and if you thought choosing the right hydroponics system was difficult, just wait until you learn all about the solutions you have to choose from.

There is a mix for lettuce, a tomato mix, a super shot mix and a mix just for blooms, there is also a one-part mix, a two-part mix and a three-part mix, and each of the mixes are available in many different brands. So how are you supposed to know which mix is the best mix for your garden?

The first thing you have to understand is that your plants are going to require a large amount of the different nutrients. These nutrients include nitrogen, potassium, sulfur, phosphorus, magnesium, and calcium. No matter what type of nutrient solution, you have to ensure that your solution contains all of these nutrients and that your plants are able to absorb them in large amounts. You also have to ensure that your solution provides each of the nutrients in perfect balance if you want your plants to grow.

On top of your nutrient rich solution needing all of the nutrients, you also have to ensure that they contain several different micro-nutrients as well. These micro-nutrients, include chlorine, copper, zinc, and boron. There are many other micro-nutrients that must be present in the solution as well, but these four are the most important.

It is important for you to know that the fertilizers you will use in a hydroponics system are much different than those you would use in traditional gardening. You want to ensure that you are only using fertilizers in your solution that have been approved for hydroponics systems, otherwise, you risk not only destroying your plants but your entire hydroponics system as well.

You get what you pay for and for this reason, it is important for you to avoid cheap nutrient solutions. If you waste your money on these cheap solutions, you will see the results in your plants so it is best if you provide your plants with the high quality solution they desire so they can produce the fruit and vegetables you desire.

The next thing you need to know is how to mix your solutions. Mixing nutrient solutions is something hydroponics growers do on a regular basis and it is also something that many growers try to take shortcuts with.

Of course, shortcuts may be tempting, especially if you have been using hydroponics for a long time. You may think you have mixed the nutrient solution so many times that you know what you are doing, but no matter how long you have been mixing the solution you need to make sure you follow the directions from beginning to end each and every time.

Hydroponics

You should also make sure that you are mixing your solution in the correct amount of water. Some people think that it will be okay for them to mix their solution in a small amount of water and then add the rest of the water later, but you have to remember your nutrient solution is in separate containers for a reason. The simple reason is because when they are not diluted properly before being mixed, they will react to each other. This can be seen as a white foam on top of your water.

You can test this by taking equal parts of your nutrient solution mix and mixing them in a small container. When you do this, you will see the natural reaction or white foam forming.

Knowing which part comes first is also very important. If you are using a two or three-part solution, you want to make sure that you begin by adding the part of the solution that contains the phosphate first. When you are using the two-part solution, it is usually the "B" part that you will use first and then the "A" part. When you are using a three-part solution, you will usually find that the phosphate is divided in between two of the parts. When this is the case, you need to pay close attention to which part has the highest amount of phosphate.

Two and three-part nutrient solutions can make the lives of some growers a bit of a hassle, but others find that mixing their own solution is quite simple and they prefer it because they are able to provide their plants with the exact nutrients they need.

Whatever nutrients you choose to use in your hydroponics systems, you need to follow the dosing guides that come with the solution. You do not want to underfeed nor overfeed your plants because as we have already learned, underfeeding them can make for weak plants and overfeeding them can cause buildup around the roots, which will lead to a toxic environment.

Stirring is very important when it comes to your nutrient solution. You cannot simply add the nutrient solution parts into the water and not mix them because it will affect the pH of your water.

One mistake many growers make is that they simply think they can mix the solution together, eyeballing the amount of solution that they put in their reservoirs, but you have to be very careful when you are measuring the amount of nutrient solution you are mixing in your water.

Mixing your solution is not difficult, but it does require you to pay attention to what you are doing and for you to be able to follow directions. You cannot use a hydroponics system without using a nutrient solution. If you are going to use a hydroponics solution, you need to take the time to think about the nutrient rich solution you are going to use in your system.

Chapter 7 : Understanding pH Levels

The ideal pH level for most hydroponics systems is going to be between 5.8 and 6.2. This is true unless you are using Rockwool as your medium, then, you will want to make sure that your pH levels are staying at about 5.5.

If your nutrient rich solution has a high pH, or is acidic, then the pH levels will be between 0 and 6.9 and if the nutrient rich solution has a low pH level, or is alkaline, then the pH levels will be between 7.1 and 14. Water, when it is pure, is neutral, which means that its pH level is 7.0.

All of this is great information, but you may be sitting there asking yourself what pH really is. When a person is measuring the pH levels in any solution, they are determining the acidity or alkalinity of said solution. These levels are determined by the amount of positive ions and negative ions that are found in the solution. Hydrogen ions are positive and hydroxyl ions are negative. This means that a nutrient solution that has more hydrogen than hydroxyl will be acidic and the nutrient solution that has more hydroxyl than hydrogen will be alkaline.

If the pH levels in your solution are not at the correct level, your plants will not be able to absorb some of the nutrients it requires for optimal growth.

There are several different ways that you can measure the pH levels of your nutrient rich solution. There are pH test kits, digital meters, and test strips. The test strips use dyes that are sensitive to pH levels and they change color when they are dipped into your nutrient rich solution. After the paper strips are dipped into the solution and they change color, they will be compared to a color chart to determine the pH levels in your nutrient solution. To use a pH test kit, you will take a small amount of your nutrient rich solution out of your reservoir, then place a few drops of the dye that comes in the kit into the solution. The dye is pH sensitive and will change the color of the liquid, then this color can be compared to a chart and will tell you the pH levels of your nutrient solution.

There is also a digital meter that you can use to check the pH levels of your nutrient rich solution. When you use the digital meter, you simply dip the electrode into the solution and it will measure the pH levels of the solution, displaying it on the display.

These meters are very accurate and they work very fast when they are properly calibrated and maintained. You have to take care of these meters or they will not function properly. You have to clean the glass electrodes and there are some that must be kept wet all of the time. You also have to calibrate these meters regularly to ensure they are working properly.

If you find that you are dealing with a high pH levels on a regular basis, you can use what is called pH down to help balance your pH levels. The opposite applies for if your pH levels are too low you can use pH up to raise your levels. It is always recommended to adjust pH levels slowly as you don't want to overdo it and keep dumping more chemicals into your nutrient solution than needed.

Chapter 8 : Temperature and Humidity

It is not enough to simply choose a hydroponics system, choose a medium, check pH levels, and choose the best lighting system when it comes to growing with hydroponics. You also have to take the temperature of the area that you are growing the plants into consideration as well as the humidity of the area.

You have to ensure that your plants are growing in the right environment to ensure maximum growth and production.

So you are probably tired of hearing this by now, but temperature and humidity are another of the most important factors that you need to pay attention to when it comes to growing with hydroponics.

Different plants are going to need different temperatures during different hours of the day so it is important for you to be able to control the environment your plants are in.

Plants that grow in the warm season such as tomatoes, peppers, melons, squash, and herbs will need a daytime temperature between 70° F to 80° F and a nighttime temperature between 60° F and 70° F with a maximum temperature of 90° F.

Plants that grow in the cooler season such as lettuce, spinach, cabbage, and green onions will need a daytime temperature between 60° F and 70° F and a nighttime temperature between 50°F and 60°F with a minimum temperature of 40° F.

Many people think that because plants seem to have a growth spurt when it is warm that they should keep their plants warm during all hours but that simply is not true. Plants need time to rest and their metabolism requires a cooler temperature during the night hours.

One of the best things you can do is to place a thermometer in the area where you are growing your plants and mark your day and night temperatures. Keep track of the temperature and be mindful of how the temperature is affecting your plants.

You may find that during the summer months, especially if you are using a grow room or are keeping your plants indoors, the temperatures are far too high for you to have healthy plants. This is often because of the lighting system. Of course, you will not want to get rid of your lighting system and we have already discussed how important the lighting is to your hydroponics system so you have to deal with the heat in another way.

The easiest and cheapest way of reducing the amount of heat in your grow room is to place a vent in the room, pushing the hot air out and replacing it with cooler air. It is important that you do not simply use a vent to remove the hot air without replacing that air with cooler air. Many beginners make this mistake, but imagine sitting in a hot house with a vent on, all of the hot air is being pushed out but no cool air is replacing that hot air. The environment is going to remain very hot and the vent is not going to benefit you at all.

When you are installing a vent, you need to remember that hot air rises, so your vent should be installed up high and the cool air will sink so it is best if your system you are using to pump in cool air is not located near the floor. You will also want to make sure that you are in complete control of the environment because you do not want the environment to jump to the opposite end of the spectrum. In other words, you do not want the grow room to become too cool for your plants to grow.

Humidity is another issue you need to think about when it comes to your hydroponics system. If you live in a humid environment, you know what it feels like, for those who do not, think about what it feels like the inside of a greenhouse. If you have ever been in a greenhouse, that feeling that you get inside there is the absolute highest amount of humidity that you would want in your hydroponics grow room. However, this is not going to give you the healthiest plants you could have.

Instead, you need to ensure that the relative humidity in your grow room is between 50% to 80% and you should aim for 50%. You have to know how humidity affects the plants and in essence, if the humidity levels are too high, then your plants will suffocate. If your plants cannot breathe properly, they are not going to be able to grow, which means that you are not going to get the yield you desire.

A very humid environment is going to cause other issues as well. Issues such as mold and mildew as well as other nasty funguses growing not only in the environment but also on the plant. Of course, this can cause many issues with the plants and can even lead to death. On the other end of the spectrum, if the humidity levels are too low, your plants are not going to be able to pollinate.

Although having too high or too low humidity can cause many serious problems when it comes to your plants, these issues are very easy to get under control. If your humidity levels are too low, all you have to do is take a trip to your local Walmart and pick up a humidifier for about 30 dollars. On the other hand, if the humidity is too high, a few fans placed in the room will help to drive out the air.

If you are growing your plants in a damp basement, a simple fan is not going to get the humidity under control. Instead, you are going to have to purchase a dehumidifier for your grow room.

If you are growing your plants outdoors, you do not have to worry about humidity and temperature, these will take care of themselves naturally.

Chapter 9 : The Growing Process

The growing process when you are using hydroponics is quite simple and does not differ too much from the traditional gardening growing process.

When you start your seeds, you will start them in a medium such as the oasis cubes. You will use whatever method you choose, placing them in the sun or under a grow light, but instead of simply watering them, you will give them the nutrient rich solution.

Once the seeds have sprouted and have taken root, you can transfer them to your hydroponics system, but you need to make sure that they are big enough for your specific system.

You do not want to place your spouts in your system only to see them washed away or drowned so you should not rush the process of getting them into your hydroponics system.

Once the plants are in the hydroponics system, they will grow just as they would if you were growing them in a traditional garden. The difference is that the plants are going to grow a lot faster than they would in a traditional garden and they are going to begin producing more fruit quicker than if they were in a traditional garden. Studies have shown that you can actually triple the amount of food that you are able to grow when you are using a hydroponics system versus traditional gardening.

That brings us to the last thing I want to cover in this chapter and that is hydroponics versus traditional gardening.

When you think about how you are growing your plants, one of the most important things people tend to think about is the pesticides. Many people choose to grow their own vegetables and fruits simply because they know the amount of pesticides that have been put on the foods they are eating.

It does no one any good to grow their own plants if they are just going to cover them with the same pesticides that are used in commercial growing. The great thing about hydroponics is that you do not have to use any pesticides. Many hydroponics systems are indoors, which prevents all pests that come from the soil and all disease. Even for those systems that are kept outside, there is no need for pesticides because since there is no dirt for the bugs and other pests to hide in, they leave the plants alone.

Another important factor that both those using hydroponics systems and traditional methods have to take into consideration is the impact of the fertilizer we are using. When you place fertilizer on your plants in a traditional garden, it does not do a lot of good. We have already talked about how the soil is depleted of nutrients, but many people think that placing fertilizer on the ground is going to help the plants absorb the nutrients they need but that really is not true. Most of the nutrients from the fertilizer get washed away with watering or rain and one of the biggest downsides to using fertilizer on your traditional garden is that you do not have any idea what nutrients you are giving to your plants.

On the other hand, when you use hydroponics, with fertilizers or nutrient rich solutions, you know that your plants are getting balanced nutrients. This nutrient rich solution is going to be washed over your roots day after day and one of the really great things about the solution is that it can be poured over plants that are in the ground each time you change your water and solution.

Hydroponics

One of the things that many people do not like about hydroponics systems is that some of them do require extra energy. Of course, traditional gardening uses the light and the energy of the sun, but when you have a hydroponics system, whether indoors or out, you are going to use more electricity. You will need to use electricity for your pumps, your lights, your timers, and many of the other parts of your system. You have to weigh the positives and the negatives when it comes to deciding to use a hydroponics system and determine if using that extra amount of electricity is worth it for you.

Another topic that many people want to know about concerning hydroponics versus traditional farming is the amount of water that is used. Many people would wrongly assume that traditional gardening uses the lowest amount of water, but the truth is that traditional gardening uses more water than hydroponics systems.

Water is used over and over again in a hydroponics system, which means using 90% less water than traditional gardening does. Hydroponics is a great way for you to grow your plants in a drought or in the desert where the conditions just do not support traditional farming.

Traditional farming is highly reliant upon the rain, which can lead to many issues. When there is a drought, it can lead to the plants simply drying out and as it was here just last year, when there is a lot of flooding, plants tend to just wash away. Traditional farming depends a lot on the land as well. This means that if you are like me and you have a large amount of land that is nothing but a rocky mess, you are not able to grow a traditional garden.

Hydroponics systems, however, do not rely on rain (unless, you are using the rain water to fill your reservoir), the outside weather, or the conditions of the soil. If you put all of this together, it means that anyone can grow a garden, not just those in the Midwest with large front yards and a good amount of rainfall.

Hydroponics also outweighs traditional farming when it comes to bringing in the bacon. Because the plants grow at least twice as fast in a hydroponics system as they would in a traditional garden, you are going to yield more fruits and vegetables. You are also going to be growing very healthy fruits and vegetables, which is what people are looking for today.

If you compare the two, traditional farming and hydroponics farming, you will quickly see that hydroponics wins out every time.

In the previous chapters, I have talked all about hydroponics, from choosing your system, to growing your food, you now have all of the information you need to ensure you know how to grow the healthiest plants possible.

In the last chapter of this book, I want to give you tips and tricks you can use to ensure your success when it comes to growing plants with a hydroponics system.

Chapter 10 : Tips and Tricks to Ensure Your Success

To finish up this book, I want to give you lots of tips and tricks that will help ensure your success in growing your plants in a hydroponics system. These are tips and tricks from experienced growers who have experimented a lot over the years and want you to be as successful as they are.

1. If you are looking to build your hydroponics system from recycled material, don't forget to check out Craigslist. So many people do their best to give away the things they do not need and you may even find an entire hydroponics system for free or for a very low price. You should also check out the local yard sale sites and you will also want to check out local yard sales. Hydroponics systems can literally be made out of anything that you find around your house or at local sales; all you have to do is be a bit creative and look for the system that works for you.

2. If you do not want to keep your hydroponics system in the house and you do not want to worry about your plants getting enough light, you can set up your hydroponics system in a greenhouse. Greenhouses are very easy to put together and you can purchase small ones for quite cheap if you do not have a lot of space. Having a greenhouse is going to take the hydroponics system out of your house, ensure that your plants are getting the right amount of light, and reduce your issues with humidity. If you do want to use a greenhouse, you need to consider how you will get electricity to your system. It is important for you to think about this in advance so that you do not get your entire system

set up in your greenhouse and then realize that you do not have any way to get electricity to your system.

3. Make sure that you know the equipment you will need for your system and why you will need it. I hope I have done a good job at explaining what you will need for your system and why you will need it, but it is important for you to know this because not knowing your system is one of the reasons many people fail at hydroponics. Many people think that they can take shortcuts with their system, cutting out vital equipment that the system needs and soon, they find out that the system will not work the way they thought it would. This often leads to discouragement and the person will give up on hydroponics, blaming the system for the issues and not realizing that they did not follow the directions. Make sure you follow the directions when it comes to your system and the equipment you will need.

4. Use a three-part hydroponics nutrient solution. The three-part nutrient solution is going to be the best for your plants, providing the right nutrients in the correct proportions. Your nutrient solution is very important when it comes to the growth and health of your plants. If you do not provide your plants with the best nutrient solution possible, you are going to find that your plants do not do well and your yields are going to be very low.

5. You should not keep your hydroponics garden outside unless the temperature is above 55° F. The great thing about a hydroponics system is that it can be moved outdoors in the summer months and indoors during the winter months. This means that you are going to be able to have healthy, fresh fruits and vegetables all year round. It is also a great idea

Hydroponics

to grow the summer foods during the summer months, when the growing season is coming to an end, clean your system, move it into the house and plant the fall foods. This will not only give you a variety of foods, but it will mean that you have less to worry about when it comes maintaining specific temperatures for your system.

6. Check your nutrient reservoir each and every day. If you have a pump in your system, it is important for you to check the pump on a regular basis because if your pump stops working, your entire system can collapse within a few hours but you also need to check the levels of your nutrient solution. If you do find that the levels are low, simply add some extra water to the reservoir. You do not want to add extra nutrient solution because the nutrients can build up on the roots of the plants and cause a toxic environment. Also, if you are continually adding nutrient solution to your reservoir, the nutrients will never deplete and you will never have a really good time to clean your system.

7. When you are cleaning your system, you need to move quickly. It is important to clean the inside of the reservoir to ensure that algae does not grow in it and deplete your nutrient solution, but you do not want to allow your plants to dry you either. Cleaning the system needs to be done at least once every 10 days and it can be something that can cause a bit of dread because of the amount of speed that is needed to clean it but once you get into a routine, it will get much easier. I would advise that before you start, you get all of your supplies together, that way you do not have to run around gathering your supplies while your plants have no nutrient rich solution available to them.

8. Minimize the amount of light that reaches your nutrient rich solution. The light is what will allow the algae to grow. If a lot of light is reaching your solution, you will have a lot of problems with algae, you will have to clean your reservoir more and you will be wasting a ton of your nutrients and doing nothing more than feeding algae.

9. Stay out of your garden after you have been in another garden or if you have been outside. This is especially true if you have your garden indoors. I stated earlier that you will not have to worry about bugs because there is no soil, but if you are in another garden that does have bugs, they can hang on to your clothes and make their way to your garden, completely destroying your plants in no time. Instead, shower and change your clothes before visiting your garden, just to make sure that you do not bring any little hitchhikers home with you to your healthy garden.

10. Never allow your pets in your garden. The reason for this is the same as the last tip, but it is also because some animals will spray or urinate on the plants simply because they smell like outdoors. They will also chew on the plants if they are able to reach them. Another reason is that you do not want your dog drinking the nutrient rich solution and you do not want his saliva in your solution. Finally, if you have a large animal or an animal that likes to climb, you run the chance of having your entire system knocked over and all of your plants, nutrient rich solution and medium spilled onto the floor.

11. Before you add any new plants to your garden that you have not grown yourself, you want to put them in quarantine for at least two weeks. You do not want any pests being brought into your hydroponics

Hydroponics

system from the greenhouse or nursery, nor do you want any diseases being brought into your system. To avoid this, simply keep the new plants away from your hydroponics system for a minimum of two weeks.

12. If you are transplanting from soil, it can seem almost impossible, but it is very easy to do. All you need to do is gently dip the roots of the plant in water, allowing the water to wash the soil away. You do not want to rub the roots because you could break them very easily and you do not want to spray them with a hose for the same reason. You do not have to worry if you cannot get every speck of soil off of the roots because as your nutrient rich solution washes over the roots, it will remove the extra bits of soil. This soil will not hurt your system as long as it is not huge clumps and it will settle to the bottom of your reservoir once the solution has rinsed over the roots.

13. Do not allow visitors into your garden. The reason for this is the same reason that you do not want to visit your garden after being outside.

14. Do not try and mix your own nutrient rich solution. It is tempting with all of the DIY recipes out there, but it is so much easier and safer for you to simply purchase the nutrient rich solution from your local gardening center. If you are mixing your own nutrient solution, you are not going to be able to guarantee your plants are getting the amount of nutrients they need. However, if you purchase the nutrient rich solution, you will know that your plants are getting what they need and you will know what they are getting.

15. Be very careful when you are adding your additives as well. You do not want to purchase cheap additives and you do not want to try and make them on your own. No matter what you are adding to your system, you want to make sure that it is regulated to ensure the health of your plants.

There are 15 tips to help ensure that you are able to be successful at growing your plants in your hydroponics system. Hydroponics are quite easy, even though they may seem very complicated when you break them apart and look at all of the different components. Not only is hydroponics growing much easier than traditional growing, but it is also much more fun. Weeding and fighting bugs is not fun, but growing healthy, vibrant food is.

Chapter 11 : Creating a Bubble Bucket

Material List
One five-gallon bucket with lid.
One roll aluminum tape (not duct tape).
One 1/2" PVC Ball Valve (inside threaded on both ends).
Two 1/2" PVC Male Adaptor **Thread x Socket**
Two 1/2" PVC Elbow for Flexible Pipe.
One 1/2" Threaded PVC Plug.
One 1/2" Threaded Coupling.
Two 1/2" Threaded PVC Adapter to Flexible Pipe.
Two 1/2" Grommets.
Four "O" Rings that fit the threads of the Male Adaptor.
One piece of 1/2" PVC Pipe
Two 1/2" PVC Tees
2' Clear Flexible Tubing with 1/2" inside diameter

Shopping list for the local pet store:
8' of Silicone Airline Tubing
2 Air stones
2 Plastic check valves
1 Air Pump

Shopping list for a hydro store:
1 6" Net Pot
1 Bag of Hydroton Pebbles

The Building Process
We don't want light to pass through the bucket, so I use aluminum tape. Duct tape won't work. Light will pass through duct tape. Also its better to tape before drilling holes. Start by taping outside of lid.

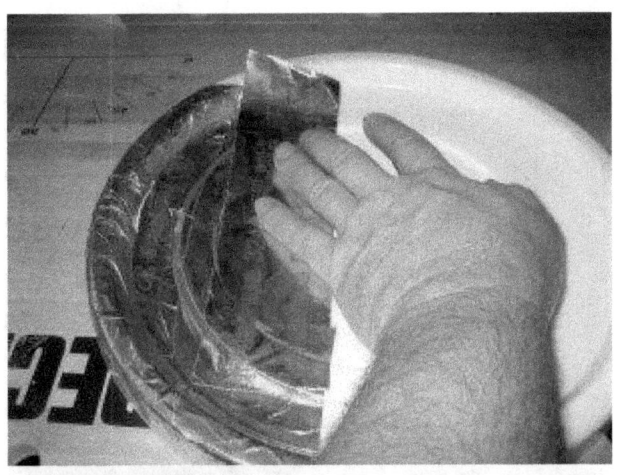

Completely tape the outside of the bucket. Do the outside bottom as well.

Hydroponics

We now need to cut a hole in the lid to fit your mesh basket. The hole has to be about 1/4" smaller then the top outside diameter of your basket. If you dont have any good hole cutting tools, you can use a razor (don't cut your fingers off). Drill/Cut your hole in the center of the lid.

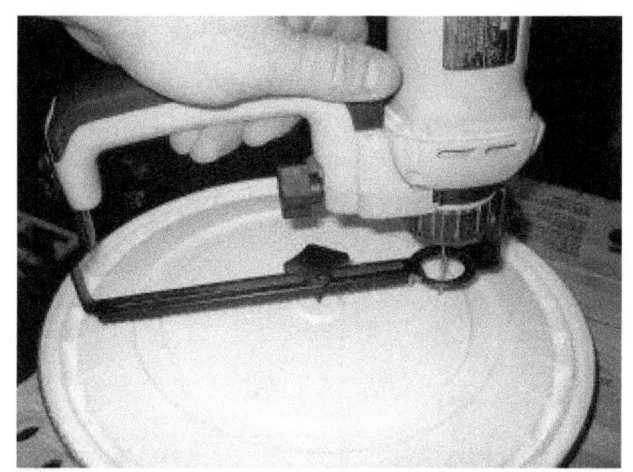

Hydroponics

Its important to know the height of your mesh basket so you can position the fill hole below the bottom of your basket. After measuring your basket height, place your lid on your bucket. Mark your fill hole location about an inch more then your basket height from the hole in your lid.

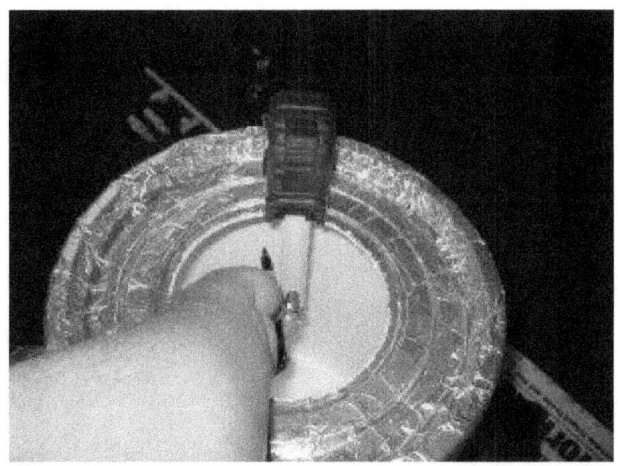

The 1/2" PVC Male Adaptor has an outside diameter of about an inch. This will be your drain, so it needs to be as close to the bottom of the bucket as possible. I measure up and mark it about 3/4" from the bottom of the bucket. If you drill to close to the bottom it will not install correct.

Hydroponics

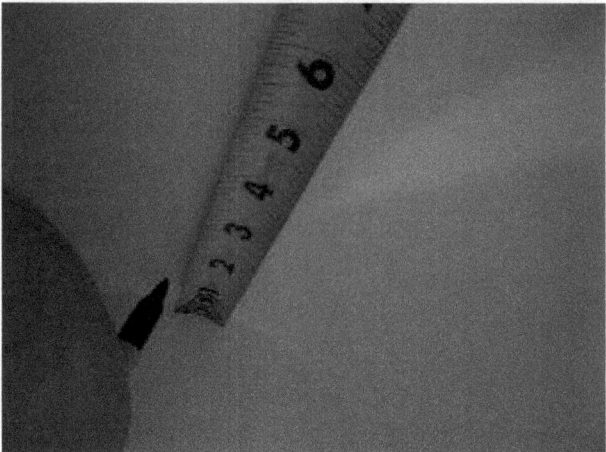

I like to have my drain and fill, in line with each other. You can put them anyplace that works with your grow. Use a small drill to make pilot holes through your bucket.

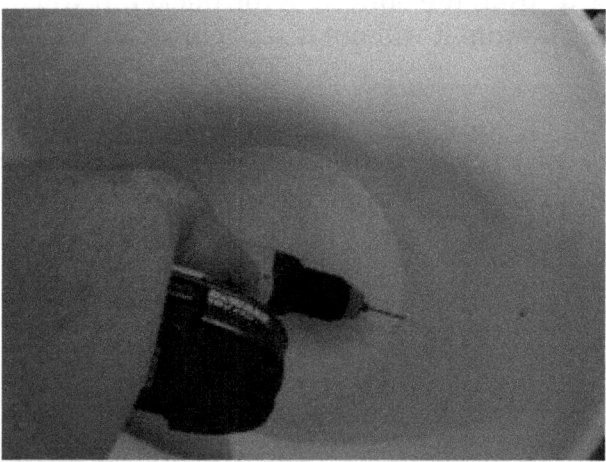

Now flip your bucket over. You should be able to see the locations of your pilot holes. Switch to a 3/4" drill bit. Anything that will make a 3/4" hole will work.

Drill out your drain and fill holes.

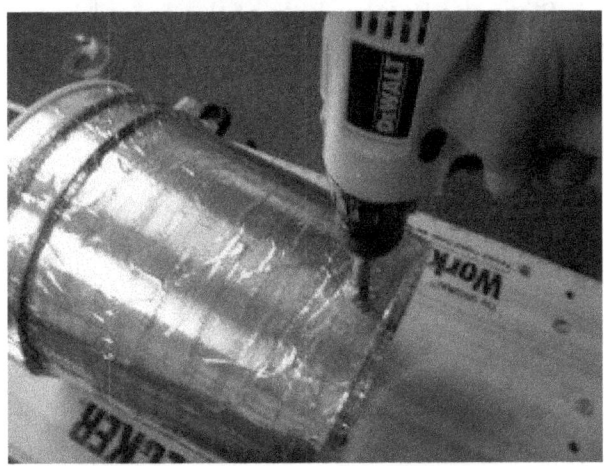

Hydroponics

To make your fluid level Indicator. We have to drill two more 3/4" holes. Place the bottom hole at the same level as the drain. Drill the top hole 1.5" from the top. You can make the top hole higher if you want.

Let's drill two holes (#7 drill bit or one slightly smaller than your airline) below the top lip on opposite sides of the bucket for the air lines.

Hydroponics

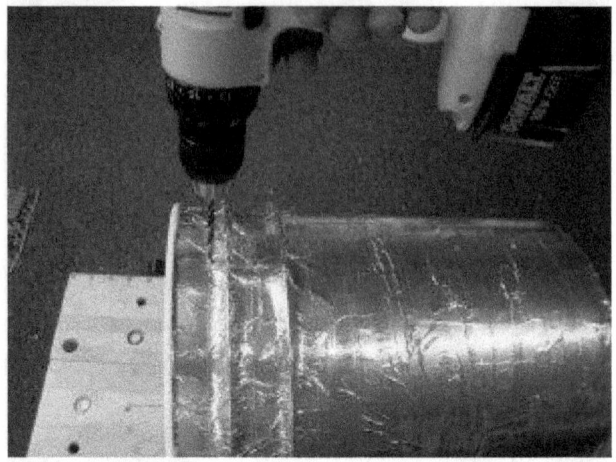

Now the fun part. Time to install all our fittings.

Place O-rings on all both 1/2" PVC Male Adaptors

Insert the male adaptors through the drain and fill holes from the inside of the bucket. It will be a tight fit.

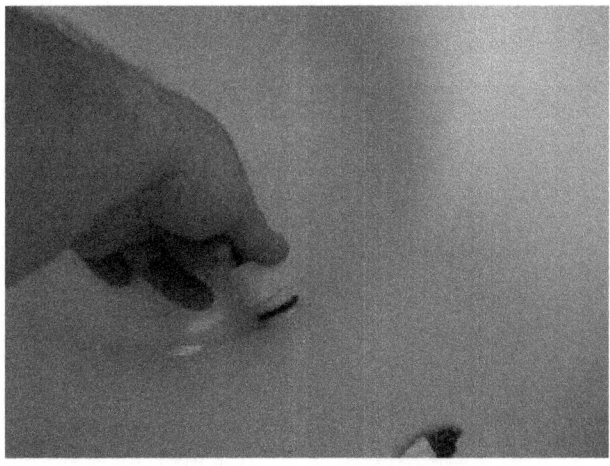

Add O-rings to the threads that stick out of the bucket. Then screw on your valve to the drain and 1/2" threaded coupling + plug to your fill.

Hydroponics

Install your rubber grommets to the 3/4" holes you made for your level indicator. Note: If you can't find grommets, you can construct this using 1/2" PVC Male Adaptor, PVC Elbow for Flexible Pipe, and two O' rings.

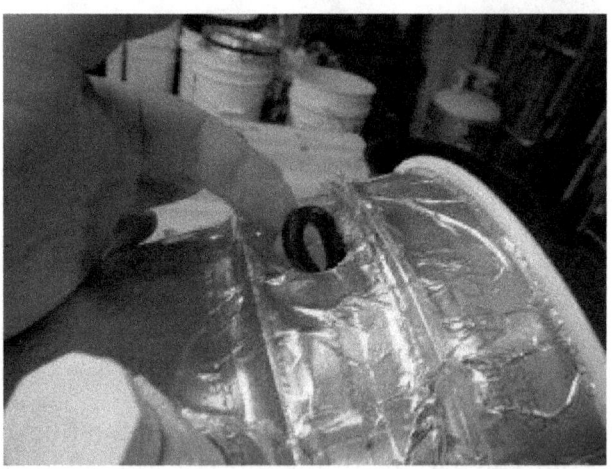

I like to cut half the barbs off one side of my tubing elbows. The cut side will go into the clear tubing. This gives me another inch or so of indicator.

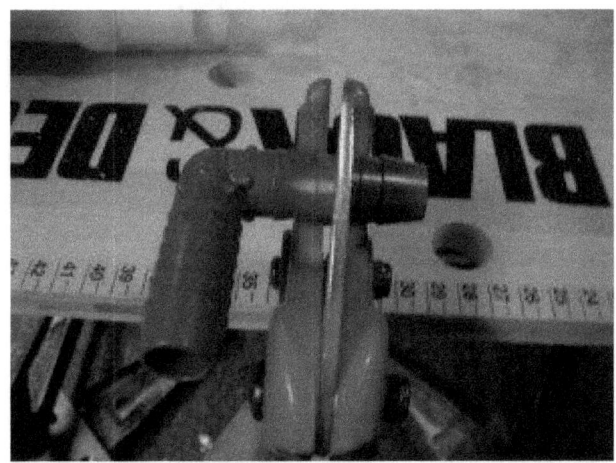

Install your two tubing elbows into your grommets. Careful not to push your grommets out of the holes you drilled. I spit on the barbs before installing them. Measure the distance between the two elbows.

Cut your clear tubing to the same distance between the two elbows.

Hydroponics

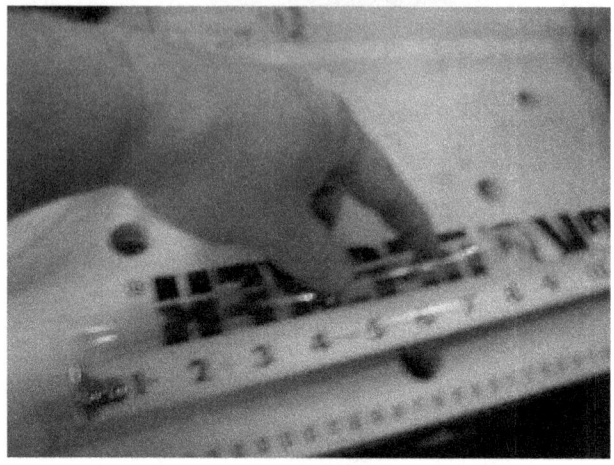

Now install the tube to your elbows.

Cut a 7.5" piece of 1/2" PVC pipe

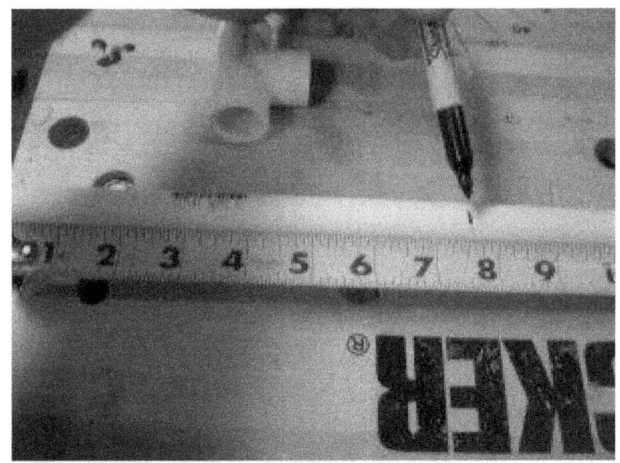

Attach a PVC Tee to each end (no glue). Using a number 7 drill bit or a bit that is just slightly smaller than your silicone airline tubing, drill two holes in your pipe. Drill close to the base of the Tee.

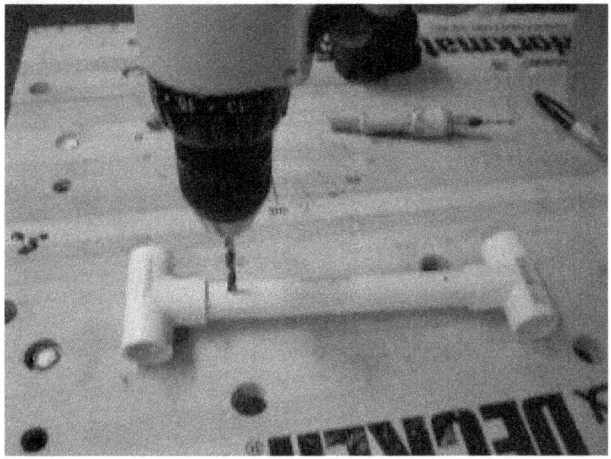

Cut about 4' of silicone airline tubing. Run your silicone airline tubing through your Tee and into your pipe then out the hole you drilled. It helps to cut a point into the end of your silicone airline to thread through the small holes.

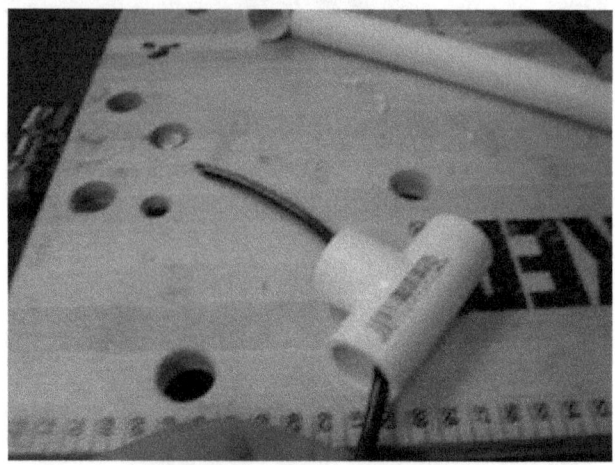

Attach your air stone and do the same thing to the other side.

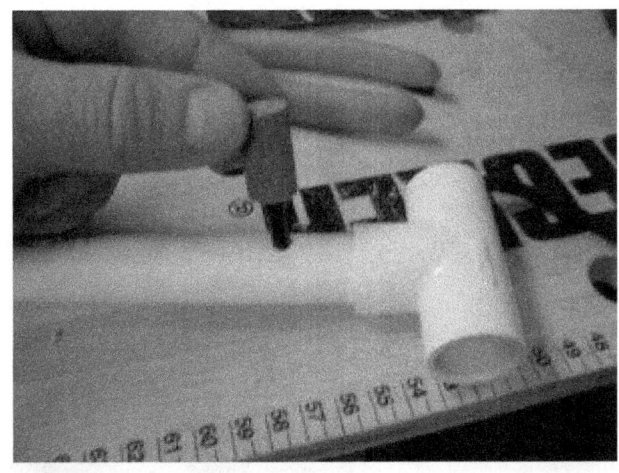

This will hold your air stones in place without adding any metal parts.

Hydroponics

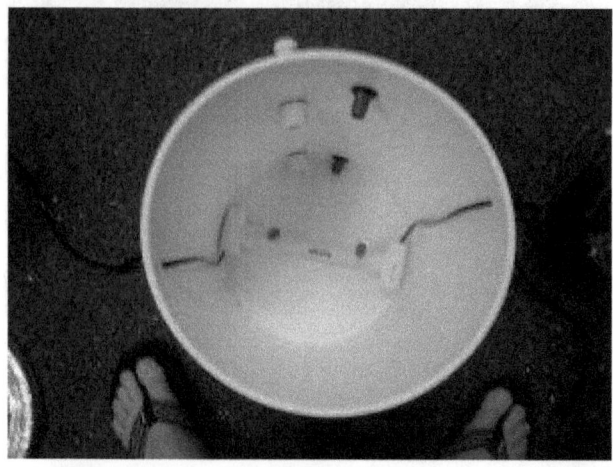

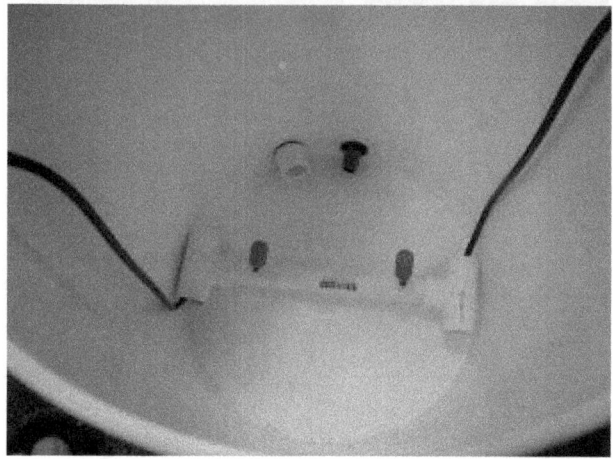

Feed the airline through the bucket. If you want your airline to be neat, you can drill small holes in the top rings of your bucket and attach zip-ties.

If you plan to have an air pump below your nutrient level, then you need to have check valves. You don't want to ruin your new pump by having water back-up into it.

Hydroponics

Now test out our new Bubble-Bucket. Look for leaks. Don't over tighten against your O-rings. If your rings smash, back up a turn or two.

Conclusion

Thank you again for downloading this book!

I hope this book was able to help you to decide exactly how you want to grow using the hydroponic method. It is definitely a challenging process to learn however once it has been mastered it can be very fulfilling. Nothing is better than walking into a room in your house and plucking off a fresh vegetable to go eat.

Since you have completed this book the next step is to create your growing system, choose your medium, lighting, nutrients, and start earning your green thumb! With time and practice you will have the indoor garden of your dreams!

If you enjoyed this book, then I'd like to ask you for a favor, would you be kind enough to leave a review for this book on Amazon? It'd be greatly appreciated!

Thank you and good luck!

www.ingramcontent.com/pod-product-compliance
Lightning Source LLC
Chambersburg PA
CBHW071330040426
42444CB00009B/2124